T0145137

CLAIRE BEAR STRONG

iUniverse books may be ordered through booksellers or by contacting:

iUniverse
1663 Liberty Drive
Bloomington, IN 47403
www.iuniverse.com
844-349-9409

Because of the dynamic nature of the Internet, any web addresses or links contained in this book may have changed since publication and may no longer be valid. The views expressed in this work are solely those of the author and do not necessarily reflect the views of the publisher, and the publisher hereby disclaims any responsibility for them.

Any people depicted in stock imagery provided by Getty Images are models, and such images are being used for illustrative purposes only. Certain stock imagery © Getty Images.

ISBN: 978-1-6632-5063-6 (sc)
ISBN: 978-1-6632-5209-8 (hc)
ISBN: 978-1-6632-5064-3 (e)

Library of Congress Control Number: 2023902251

Print information available on the last page.

iUniverse rev. date: 03/10/2023

Claire BEAR STRONG

In hopes of inspiring others who may be trolling through their own difficult journey, I'd like to dedicate this book to our daughter, Claire. Life may not always go as you pictured it, but your outlook and bravery has taught us all so much! Perspective is everything, and I hope this book helps many others.-Love, Mom

MEGHAN LAMBREMONT

When Claire was 3, she was diagnosed with the Big "C".

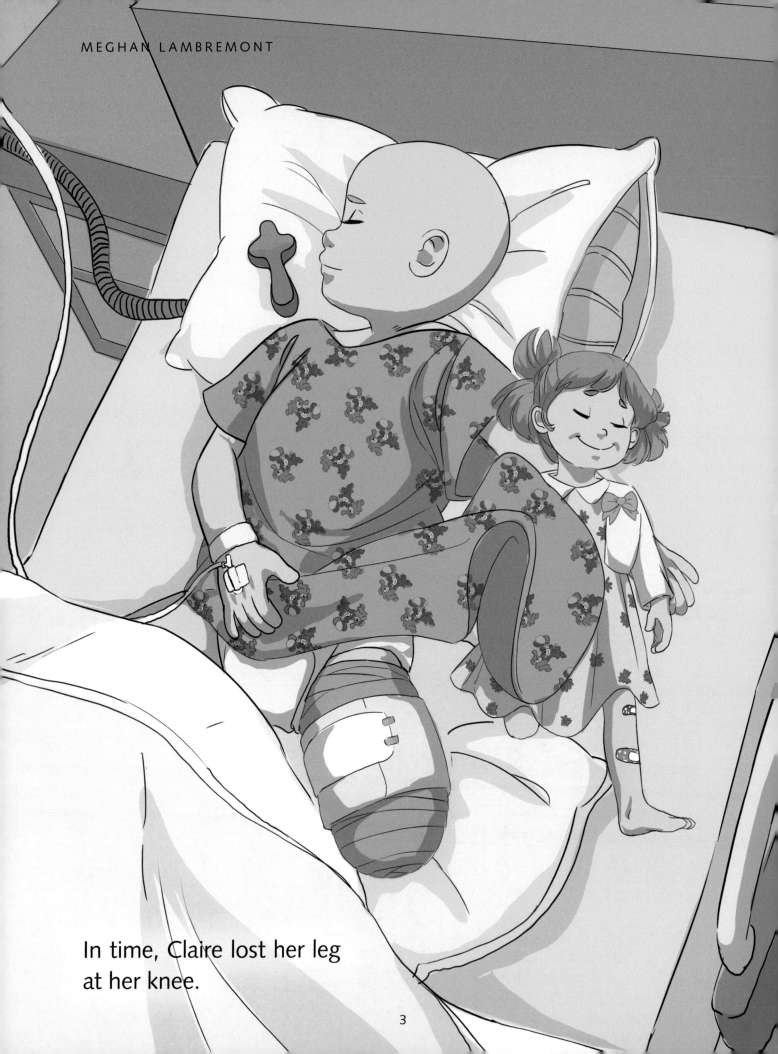

In time, Claire lost her leg
at her knee.

But this never stopped her from feeling free.

MEGHAN LAMBREMONT

Whether a foot or a
blade, Claire can now
choose her leg!

From Ariel, the Mermaid
to hearts so bright,

Claire has always been
a ray of light!

You can be too!

Let me show you all
that Claire can do...

MEGHAN LAMBREMONT

Claire can run.

Claire can swim and enjoy her day in the sun.

Claire can dance and skip.

Or do cartwheels and flips.

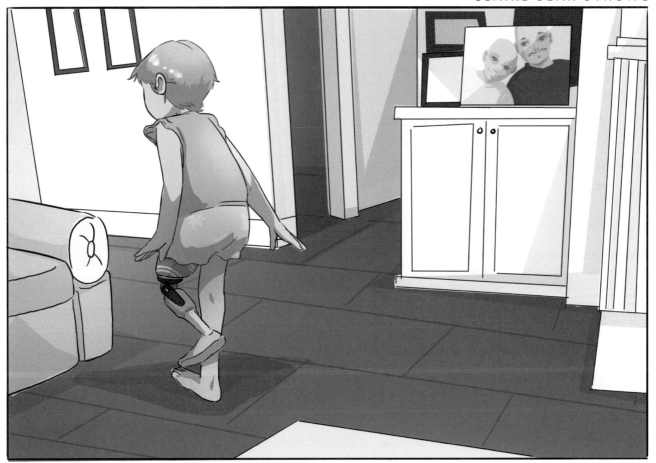

Claire can climb and jump however she likes

And even ride scooters and bikes!

From playing ball or climbing a wall,

Claire can still do it all!

Claire is BRAVE.

Claire is STRONG.

Claire is INSPIRING.

Don't get me wrong, her journey was tough, her journey was long...

But Claire always stayed Claire Bear STRONG!

Printed in the United States
by Baker & Taylor Publisher Services